Chewy Hughie

Written by Jane Clarke

Illustrated by Sarah McConnell

Collins

All Hughie does is chew, chew, chew.

Whatever are we going to do?

He chews up toys, he chews up bones.

He chews up shoes and mobile phones.

4

He chews his bed, he chews his bowls.
He chews up all our toilet rolls.

He chews our dirty underwear.
Chewy Hughie doesn't care.

He chews the paper and the mail.
When Mum says "NO!", he wags his tail.

He chews the chairs and both settees.
He chews our books and DVDs.
He chews the carpets and the doors.
Nothing's safe from Hughie's jaws.

Whatever are we going to do?
All Hughie does is chew, chew, **chew**.

Outside, he chews up grass and trees,
flowers, flies and bumblebees.

He chews up Grandad's stick and hat ...

... he tries to chew up Granny's cat.

Mum says, "Keep an eye on Hughie!"
He's in my room, but he's still chewy.

He's found a pack of bubble gum.
Hughie's chewing it for fun.

14

All Hughie does is chew, chew, chew ...

... now his jaws are stuck like glue.

Chewy Hughie's in big trouble.
He's inside a huge, pink bubble.

Hughie, you have got to stop.
Don't chew, Hughie, you'll go ...

Now Hughie doesn't chew, chew, chew.
Whatever is he going to do?

A story map

Getting creative

- If your child's enjoyed reading about *Chewy Hughie*, they could try making up another adventure for him.

- They could start by planning what might happen in another story, when he can't stop digging.

- They could draw a cartoon strip for the new story. This will help children to plan the story and use their imagination to talk about new events.

- Once they've got a plan, encourage them to start telling the story, using the cartoons to help.

Other books at Level 3:

Fiction	Non-fiction
Twinkle, Twinkle Firefly	*What's that Building?*
Mountain Mona	*Unusual Traditions*
Chewy Hughie	*How to be a Knight in 10 easy stages*